## THE FATHER AND THE YOUNGEST SON

In Jesus' third story, a father with enough wealth to own land, animals, and servants had two sons. The youngest came to him to request his share of the inheritance: "Father, give me my share of the estate" (Luke 15:12). It is a short statement that does not seem to say much about their relationship or about either one of them. However, as it was the case with all the parables, Jesus used language and experiences that his listeners could understand. They could "hear between the lines" and understand the subtle points being made.

In the time of Jesus, a father's authority was like that of a king. The children were his property, and they depended on him for financial security and social standing. Families lived together and belonged to the father's household. It was only when the father had blessed his children and then passed away that each son was able to start his own household, with the oldest son becoming the new patriarch of the clan.

In the story, the younger son was, in fact, asking for his independence, for his freedom. The younger son wanted the freedom to make his own decisions, to live his life the way he wanted—a desire that opposed the values of the culture at the time. (In Jesus' time, connection to and dependence on the family and the father was a far more important value than freedom.) The younger son's demand also meant that the younger son could not wait for his father's death, when the inheritance would have been divided. In other words, his insistence showed a lack of love for his father.

In making that request, then, the younger son dishonored his father and his father's household. He forced his father to make a difficult choice. Typically, the society of the time resolved such a problem by banishment —kicking the child out. The younger son deserved to be expelled from his father's household without inheritance or family.

QUESTIONS FOR REFLECTION:

*In our day, the search for independence is highly valued.*

*How can we continue to search for independence while at the same time remain faithful to and trustful of God's grace?*

## A PSALM FOR COMFORT

Knowing that our trust is placed in a God who cares, who listens, and who acts is a source of great comfort. When Jesus returned to the Father, he promised to not leave us alone. He sent the Holy Spirit to live with and in us, to be the divine presence with us. Our confidence and comfort are made clear in Psalm 27:1-3, 13-14:

> *The Lord is my light and my salvation—whom shall I fear? The Lord is the stronghold of my life—of whom shall I be afraid?*
>
> *When the wicked advance against me to devour me, it is my enemies and my foes who will stumble and fall.*
>
> *Though an army besiege me, my heart will not fear; though war break out against me, even then I will be confident. ...*
>
> *I remain confident of this: I will see the goodness of the Lord in the land of the living.*
>
> *Wait for the Lord; be strong and take heart and wait for the Lord.*

(Also see Psalms 42 and 130.)

## A PRAYER FOR PRODIGALS

*Infinitely wise and good Father,*

*As we hurt you by our own rebellion, we are hurt by the rebellion of those we love. So just as you forgive us and accept us back to you, help us to be able to forgive and accept those loved ones who hurt us. Give us your vision, your compassion, and your love, and give us your comfort.*

*We also ask for those loved ones who are rebelling against you and us: Keep them safe from the evil in the world, guard their hearts from hurting others or themselves, and let them know that you are close and ready to hear their cries.*

*When the time is right, we ask that you take them back and bring them back to us. And we ask for the wisdom to recognize your timing; when that time arrives, may our hearts be ready to run to them, embrace them, and celebrate their return with joy and passion.*

*We ask all of these things, trusting in your compassion, knowing that you are a good and merciful God. And we ask because you've already shown us your great love by sending your own Son, Jesus Christ. In his name, we pray. Amen.*

## A PSALM FOR SADNESS AND SORROW

For parents of prodigals, sadness and sorrow well up from a deep sense of loss. But we must never forget that we believe in the God of the impossible. Even if we think a person is lost, God is the Good Shepherd who leaves the flock to find just one small, weak sheep. This is how our trust is tested and made stronger. "Blessed is the one who trusts in the LORD" (Ps. 40:4)! Psalm 42:1-5 provides solace:

> *As the deer pants for streams of water, so my soul pants for you, my God.*
>
> *My soul thirsts for God, for the living God. When can I go and meet with God?*
>
> *My tears have been my food day and night, while people say to me all day long, "Where is your God?"*
>
> *These things I remember as I pour out my soul: how I used to go to the house of God under the protection of the Mighty One with shouts of joy and praise among the festive throng.*
>
> *Why, my soul, are you downcast? Why so disturbed within me? Put your hope in God, for I will yet praise him, my Savior and my God.*

(Also see Psalms 43 and 88.)

## A PSALM FOR PROTECTION

We live in a dangerous world, one in which even those who seek peace and tranquility can be found by violence and pain. However, our God is the creator of all things. He is more than capable and willing to care for us. Our fears and anxieties will find relief when we trust that God will care for us and ours. Psalm 91:1-4 confirms this:

> *Whoever dwells in the shelter of the Most High will rest in the shadow of the Almighty.*
>
> *I will say of the LORD, "He is my refuge and my fortress, my God, in whom I trust."*
>
> *Surely he will save you from the fowler's snare and from the deadly pestilence.*
>
> *He will cover you with his feathers, and under his wings you will find refuge; his faithfulness will be your shield and rampart.*

(Also see Psalms 121 and 145.)

## GRACE AND REBELLION

The father's response to the younger son was unexpected: "So he [the father] divided his property between them" (Luke 15:12). The father's reaction must have provoked much confusion in Jesus' audience. It wasn't the right response. The younger son's insolence should have been met with a strong, negative reaction. But the father gave the younger son what he wanted.

The younger son left his father's house and, predictably, squandered all he had. As Jesus' listeners expected, the son's foolishness led him to a life of misery and humiliation. Eventually, his only option was to take care of pigs. Jews did not eat pork because they considered pigs unclean. For a Jew to be taking care of pigs was the ultimate degradation. The younger son had touched bottom.

But in time, the son's own suffering broke down his pride. In a moment of insight, he became wise: "I will set out and go back to my father and say to him: Father, I have sinned against heaven and against you. I am no longer worthy to be called your son; make me like one of your hired servants" (Luke 15:18–19).

QUESTIONS FOR REFLECTION:

*What are some ways to demonstrate true repentance and ask another person for forgiveness?*

*What does the younger son's behavior teach us about repentance?*

## AN UNEXPECTED ENCOUNTER

The son headed home, humbled and humiliated, with sorrow and newfound wisdom. Jesus' audience, the Pharisees especially, likely imagined that justice was about to be served. The father would surely act with a firm hand over his son.

However, as soon as his father saw him at a distance, the father "was filled with compassion for him; he ran to his son, threw his arms around him and kissed him" (Luke 15:20). Imagine, a dignified father taking off to meet his rebellious son, the one who had dishonored him and squandered his wealth! In Jesus' time, dignified people in Middle Eastern cultures did not run. Running was fit for servants, not for the masters of the home. But compassion moved the father, not justice, not revenge, not pride.

With humility and wisdom, the younger son apologized to the father. However, the father ignored his son's apology—along with his dirty clothes and body. Instead, he embraced his son and called to his servants to prepare a welcome fit for a most honored guest. Jesus made clear the father's reasoning for the celebration: "For this son of mine was dead and is alive again; he was lost and is found" (Luke 15:24).

Jesus' Story of the Lost Son

# THE PARABLE OF THE PRODIGAL SON

ROSE PUBLISHING

# OUR PRODIGALS

We all have either loved, known, or been a prodigal child—someone who has rebelled against parents and God and set out on a path of destruction. Whether it's fear and worry for a young adult flinging away the faith in which he or she was raised, or the ache of a friend's midlife crisis of identity and faith, the prodigals in our lives can bring up some of the deepest questions in our own faith. The parable of the Lost Son (or the Prodigal Son, as it is also known) provides a fresh viewpoint that can help us see those prodigal children from God's perspective, bringing God's grace to calm our fears, overcome our anxieties, and soften our hearts for all those prodigals that cross our paths.

## THE PARABLE OF THE LOST SON

Chapter 15 of the Gospel of Luke begins with the Pharisees and the teachers of the law leveling a criticism at Jesus: "This man welcomes sinners and eats with them" (Luke 15:2). Jesus responds to his accusers with three stories:

| PARABLE | DESCRIPTION | REFERENCE |
|---|---|---|
| **Lost Sheep** | A shepherd rejoices over finding his one lost sheep. | Luke 15:1–7 |
| **Lost Coin** | A woman searches diligently until she finds her one lost coin. | Luke 15:8–10 |
| **Lost Son** | A rebellious son is lost and then found. | Luke 15:11–32 |

In these powerful stories, Jesus calls the Jewish leaders to join him in the joy of finding that which had been lost. Jesus could not be any clearer: "I tell you that in the same way there will be more rejoicing in heaven over one sinner who repents than over ninety-nine righteous persons who do not need to repent" (Luke 15:7).

Although the Jews at that time expected a Messiah who would save them from the Roman domination, Jesus had come to find the lost, those who needed God at a more basic, intimate level. Those who already had that connection with God should have desired for all others to find that connection. Jesus came to make it possible for all to come to God. This truth should have made the righteous rejoice. Instead, they were judgmental and harsh in their criticisms.

## TWO DIFFERENT RESPONSES

The father's response to his older son was disarming: "My son,...you are always with me, and everything I have is yours. But we had to celebrate and be glad, because this brother of yours was dead and is alive again; he was lost and is found" (Luke 15:31–32). In his anger, the elder brother treated his brother like a mere object by referring to him as "this son of yours" (15:30). That is, he treated him as less than what he was. (It is easier to mistreat or stay angry with someone if we can think of that person as less than what the person is: a brother, a son, or, even, a human at all.) But the father counters "this son of yours" with "this brother of yours (15:32)." The father made it clear that material possessions were not at the center of his older son's anger ("everything I have is yours"). Nor was the problem the lack of his older son's significant presence in his life ("you are always with me"). Rather, the problem was that his older son's heart had hardened and become unable to see his brother for who he was. The older brother had lost his compassion. To be compassionate with others, we need to see them for who they are, not who we think they should be or what we think they should do.

## TWO REBELLIOUS ATTITUDES

Jesus wanted to reveal to his listeners two basic rebellious attitudes that separate and hinder us from coming to the Father:

### 1. THE YOUNGER SON: OPEN REBELLION

In the parable of the Lost Son, the younger brother rebelled in a way that is easy to recognize. His rebellion led him to a path of self-destruction. This rebellion is easy to see and easy to feel hurt by. Today, we often refer to prodigal children as those who have openly rebelled against their parents and the teachings of their church.

Throughout the history of Israel, open rebellion was a central problem. Israel rebelled when it refused to accept the terms of the covenant, the agreement that God made with their ancestors. They rebelled by worshiping other gods, by doing violence and injustice to the weak among themselves, by ignoring the warnings of God's prophets and killing them, and by refusing to accept God's sovereignty. According to the prophets, Israel's own rebellion against God led directly to Israel being conquered by the Assyrians and the Babylonians, the destruction of the Jerusalem temple and the city, and the exile of many of the people from the land.

# AVOIDING GIVING IN TO ANGER

Unfortunately, our emotional hurts can make us angry and make us act in ways that might surprise us. If we let our pain dominate our thoughts and feelings, we might end up destroying relationships or even people. When faced with prodigal children, the kind of pain we experience is deep and powerful. So our reaction can potentially cause great damage that might be very difficult to resolve, if it is not kept in check.

One way we can show our trust and commitment is by learning to wait patiently for God to act. In the story of the two sons, the father did not go out chasing after his younger son. He waited wisely and patiently. But, as soon as he saw his son coming back, he ran and embraced him with love and acceptance. Despite the emotional grief and injured pride—another possible cause for anger—we must always be ready to embrace our prodigal children, even if they are not fully ready to come back to us and to God. Even a step in the right direction needs to be acknowledged. We should not hold back our love until prodigals fully turn around, because God works in ways we can't always perceive. But, like the watchmen awaiting the morning (see Ps. 130:6), we must always be ready to recognize God's actions and be willing to rejoice in his actions and their effects.

# PRAYERS FOR THOSE WHO WAIT

When we are overwhelmed with strong emotions and feel lost in grief or despair, it is difficult to pray. Words seem to evade us, our thoughts wander aimlessly, and we seem incapable of concentration. The psalms are filled with prayers that we can use for those times, especially to remind ourselves that God is listening, even if he seems to have turned his face away from us. The Father loves us and is compassionate beyond measure, and God will never forsake us nor ignore us. We can approach the throne of the Great King with confidence because the path has been prepared for us: his Son, Jesus, leads us to the presence of the Father, and the Holy Spirit gives us words that are appropriate to address our King.

## A PSALM FOR WORRY, ANXIETY, AND ANGUISH

Matthew 7:13-14 provides an image of the two paths that people can choose between. Choosing life with God leads to life. Choosing life away from God leads to destruction and death. Because parents of prodigals are unsure of which path their prodigals will ultimately choose, they endure much worry, anxiety, and anguish. For those times, a prayer like the one in Psalm 40:1-5 can be helpful:

> *I waited patiently for the LORD; he turned to me and heard my cry.*
>
> *He lifted me out of the slimy pit, out of the mud and mire;*
> *he set my feet on a rock and gave me a firm place to stand.*
>
> *He put a new song in my mouth, a hymn of praise to our God.*
> *Many will see and fear the LORD and put their trust in him.*
>
> *Blessed is the one who trusts in the LORD, who does not look to the proud, to those who turn aside to false gods.*
>
> *Many, LORD my God, are the wonders you have done, the things you planned for us. None can compare with you; were I to speak and tell of your deeds, they would be too many to declare.*

(Also see Psalms 23, 55, 91, 102, and 145.)

## THE OTHER PRODIGAL SON

Jesus' audience might have been very puzzled by the unusual and perhaps even culturally unacceptable response of the father. And they might have also imagined that the story would end on this happy note: the younger son was back after having learned his lesson, the father had received him back, and everyone was happy. However, the climax of the story was still to come.

After the reconciliation between the younger son and his father, the story's missing character appears: the older son who had stayed home with his father, the son who was working out in the fields when his brother returned. Imagine his surprise when he heard music and celebration. After finding out the reason for the festivities, "the older brother became angry and refused to go in" (Luke 15:28). We can almost see Jesus' audience nodding their heads in sympathy for the older brother's anger. In fact, the older brother explained it to his father:

> "ALL THESE YEARS I'VE BEEN SLAVING FOR YOU AND NEVER DISOBEYED YOUR ORDERS. YET YOU NEVER GAVE ME EVEN A YOUNG GOAT SO I COULD CELEBRATE WITH MY FRIENDS." Luke 15:29

It only seems right that things in life should work like this: If I am a good person, life should treat me well. If I am an evil person, life should treat me accordingly. That seems reasonable and fair and makes sense. Why should the "bad" brother be rewarded with a reception fit for a king? Why shouldn't the "good" brother have expected better treatment from his father? Our sympathy lies with the older brother.

### QUESTIONS FOR REFLECTION:

*Has it ever occurred to you that you think you deserve happiness and wellbeing merely because you are a good person?*

*Which stories in the Bible suggest that life doesn't always work this way?*

### QUESTIONS FOR REFLECTION:

*Forgiveness in the story is placed in the context of reconciliation—the joy that reconciliation produces.*

*Have you ever experienced this sort of joy, the type that makes all anger and hurt feelings and pride disappear? Briefly describe your experience.*

# THREE KINDS OF PRODIGALS

| | THE YOUNGER SON | THE FATHER | THE OLDER SON |
|---|---|---|---|
| **Initial Actions** | • Rejects his father's love<br>• Dishonors his father and family<br>• Rebels against his father<br>• Lives an immoral life | • Listens to his son's request<br>• Grants his son's request and gives him his portion of the inheritance | • Remains silent and absent from the discussion |
| **Following Actions** | • Is humbled by his own mistakes<br>• Returns to humbly ask his father's forgiveness | • Runs to receive his younger son<br>• Receives his younger son as an honored guest and celebrates his return with a feast<br>• Invites his older son to join in the celebration<br>• Leaves the invitation open for his older son | • Feels anger and outrage, which prevent him from joining the celebration<br>• Exhibits a form of rebellion by rejecting his brother and his father's love |

ROSE PUBLISHING

© 2015 Bristol Works, Inc.
Rose Publishing, Inc.
17909 Adria Maru Lane
Carson, CA 90746 U.S.A.
email: info@rose-publishing.com
www.rose-publishing.com

*Rose Publishing has more than 100 Bible reference pamphlets.*



Register your pamphlet at www.rose-publishing.com/register

**Author:** Benjamin Galan, MTS, ThM, Professor of Old Testament Hebrew and Literature.

RELIGION/Biblical Studies/New Testament

ISBN-13: 978-159636-961-0

Stock #297X The Parable of the Prodigal Son pamphlet
Retailers: Package of 5 pamphlets = Stock #298X (ISBN-13: 978-159636-965-8)

## THREE PRODIGALS

In the parable of the Lost Son, then, there is more than one prodigal: (1) the younger son who foolishly spent his share of the inheritance; (2) the father who gave of his love and compassion freely and abundantly; and (3) the older brother who spent his own life trying to earn his father's approval and blessings but was unable to truly love him and his brother.

Although not stated, Jesus invited his listeners then and his believers now to become prodigal like the father. That means we are to become compassionate toward those who go away either in search of something or in rebellion, and welcome them back with joy and love. We are to become compassionate and open to those who have spent their lives trying to earn favor and who might be unaware of their own need for rescuing.

## OUR PRODIGAL CHILDREN

When children decide to rebel and go their own way, Christian parents experience two kinds of hurt: one for the rebellion itself and its immediate consequences, and the other for the possible future, eternal consequences. For parents, the thought of their children getting hurt causes much anxiety and worry. And the thought of children endangering their eternal destiny by rebelling and moving away from God causes even greater anxiety and grief.

The parable of the Lost Son does not give parents instructions or steps for dealing with the anxiety of having prodigal children, but it does invite parents to rest in an attitude of trust. As many of the psalms teach us, the basic attitude to have in times of grief or gratitude or joyful worship is trust—trust that God, the creator of all things, the redeemer of Israel, the rock of his people, and the sure safe port in the midst of the storm, is trustworthy and deserves our trust.

### PRODIGAL

The story in Luke 15 is commonly known as the parable of the Prodigal Son. For those familiar with the story, "prodigal" is often used to refer to a person who walks away from the faith and a good, clean life. But a dictionary definition of "prodigal" also refers to lavish or excessive spending or giving.

- The younger son was surely prodigal with the wealth he inherited, spending it carelessly and foolishly.
- Some have suggested that the real prodigal person in this story is the father, because he gave of himself and his possessions recklessly and excessively.
- Others feel that the older son is a prodigal, because his excessive pursuit of his father's approval and favor ultimately led to resentment.

## JESUS' INVITATION TO TRUST

How is trusting in God any help when children leave home to follow paths that we parents know will lead to dangerous and evil ways, even possibly to death? There are three lessons from the parable to keep in mind:

**Jesus invites us to join** in the joy of the father when those who are lost are found. And he invites us to accept those prodigals just as they are, to embrace them with open arms and loving hearts.

**Jesus invites us to act** like the father—to be compassionate and loving, to accept those who have gone away from the life of the church or were never on that path, and to receive them with joy and hope *just as they are*.

**Jesus invites us to trust** in God. Trusting God is a demanding and difficult activity. We live in a world where we have experienced much betrayal and many hurts. It is hard to trust, because often when we do, our trust can be used against us. Then we might become cynical. Trusting after being hurt takes courage. But God is trustworthy. That means that we can be assured that our trust is in good hands, that our vulnerability will not be used against us but *for* us. When we trust God, we can be absolutely sure that God is for us.

## 2. THE OLDER SON: LACK OF COMPASSION

In the parable of the Lost Son, the older son showed a lack of compassion. His outrage eclipsed his compassion for his younger brother. The older brother assumed that because he had been good and obedient, he should have been treated differently. The people of Israel demonstrated a similar serious lack of compassion for those who were weak or not part of the covenant.

| OLDER SON | RESULT | ISRAEL |
|---|---|---|
| His sense of entitlement and self-righteousness | Unable to be compassionate and rejoice at the return of his brother. Anger at his father. | Though God called Jonah to prophesy to the Assyrians in Nineveh, Jonah did not want them to repent; he wanted God to wipe them out. The contrast was meant to shame the Israelites back to God in humility and obedience. |
| His sense of justice | Unable to understand his father's reaction or his brother's need for reconciliation and a new beginning. | "He has shown you, O mortal, what is good. And what does the LORD require of you? To act justly and to love mercy and to walk humbly with your God." —Micah 6:8 |
| His lack of love | A heart of stone, unwilling to be transformed and softened to produce compassion and empathy. Anger at his brother. | "I [the LORD] will give you a new heart and put a new spirit in you; I will remove from you your heart of stone and give you a heart of flesh." —Ezekiel 36:26 |

Jesus' teaching that he was offering in a parable to his audience was this: The refusal of the Jews to accept God's calling to be shaped as a people to become a blessing to all the nations was a form of rebellion. They were unwilling to accept God's mighty acts of salvation in Jesus and be part of that new reality.

In the father's place, the older son would have given the foolish younger brother exactly what he deserved. And perhaps that seems to be what is just and fair. But in love and compassion, the father extended grace, and in his wisdom, he rejoiced for the return of a lost son.

Indeed, grace is exactly what the younger son needed. Grace is what we all need, whether we are at the heights of our strength and success or in the depths of despair and grief. From grace springs acceptance, compassion, forgiveness, and restitution. And grace itself springs from love.